O/11

FEB 2 3 2011

11/14

15|15

ELK GROVE VILLAGE PUBLIC LIBRARY

3 1250 00935 6522

19

W9-BNT-593

Discarded By Elk Grove
Village Public Library

ELK GROVE VILLAGE PUBLIC LIBRARY
1001 WELLINGTON AVE
ELK GROVE VILLAGE, IL 60007
(847) 439-0447

LET IT BLOW!
LEARN ABOUT AIR

BY JULIA VOGEL

The Child's World®

Published by The Child's World®
1980 Lookout Drive • Mankato, MN 56003-1705
800-599-READ • www.childsworld.com

ACKNOWLEDGMENTS
The Child's World®: Mary Berendes, Publishing Director
Content Consultant: Julian Marshall, PhD, Professor of Environmental Engineering
    University of Minnesota
The Design Lab: Design and production
Red Line Editorial: Editorial direction

PHOTO CREDITS: Tomasz Nieweglowski/iStockphoto, cover, 1, 3 ; Zhang Bo/iStockphoto,
5; Fotolia, 7 (top), 10; Brett Hillyard/iStockphoto, 7 (bottom); iStockphoto, 8, 15 (top), 17
(top); Jean-Michel Pouget/Fotolia, 9; Jane Yamada, 11, 23; Chris White/Fotolia, 13 (top);
Conny Sjostrom/Fotolia, 13 (bottom); Jeanne Hatch/Fotolia, 15 (bottom); Ann Worthy/
iStockphoto, 17 (bottom); Eileen Hart/iStockphoto, 19; NASA, 21

Copyright © 2011 by The Child's World®
All rights reserved. No part of this book may be reproduced or utilized in
any form or by any means without written permission from the publisher.

LIBRARY OF CONGRESS CATALOGING-IN-PUBLICATION DATA
  Vogel, Julia.
    Let it blow! : learn about air / by Julia Vogel ; illustrated by Jane Yamada.
      p. cm.
    ISBN 978-1-60253-509-1 (library bound : alk. paper)
    1. Air—Juvenile literature. I. Yamada, Jane, ill. II. Title.
    QC161.2.V64 2010
    551.5—dc22   2010010976

Printed in the United States of America in Mankato, Minnesota.
July 2010
F11538

CONTENTS

Air All Around

Breathe it.

Blow it.

Fan it.

Feel it in your hair.

Air is all around us.

It is a **gas**.

Do you like to blow the seeds off dandelions? ▶

4

Moving air is **wind**.

Wind pushes clouds across the sky.

Wind rattles leaves.

It makes ocean waves.

Wind sweeps down mountains and across deserts.

It flows around Earth.

Wind makes clouds move. ▶

Wind makes waves, too. ▶

Hot Air, Cold Air

Heat changes air.

It makes air take up more space.

Warm air gets lighter and lighter.

It rises higher in the sky.

Hot air makes balloons float. ▶

People blow up a hot air balloon. ◀

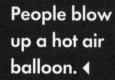

Cold air takes up less space.

It gets heavier and sinks.

When warm air floats up,
colder air rushes in below it.

That rush is the wind.

Warm air rises.
Cool air sinks. ▶

Moving air
makes wind. ◀

10

The strongest winds are swirling **tornadoes**. Roaring **hurricanes** also bring powerful winds. Tornadoes can blow down houses. Hurricanes can rip apart towns.

Sometimes air is still.
Leaves do not rattle.
Flags hang limp.
But air is always there.

A tornado looks like a cloud with a cone shape hanging down. ▶

This lake is calm because there is no wind. ▶

13

Floating on Air

Moving or still, air has the power to lift.
Kites dance in gusty winds.

Look at a sunbeam. Can you see
tiny specks floating in the light?
Air carries many small things
wherever it goes.
Seeds, dust, and smoke
float with the air.
Ah-choo!

Air lifts kites high
into the sky. ▶

Air makes dust
dance in the
sunlight. ◀

14

Air also carries smells.

Bits of food or **pollution** float through air to your nose.

Mmmmm! You might smell warm cookies.

Or yuck! Here comes the garbage truck.

Cars give off pollution that smells bad. ▸

Spring brings wonderful smells! ▸

Air even carries sound. *Pop!*
A burst balloon makes sound waves.
The waves ripple through air to your
ears. Sound waves must ripple through
something. That something is air.

Do you ever
blow bubbles?
When they
pop, air carries
the sound to
your ears. ▶

Incredible Air

Air wraps around Earth like a fluffy blanket. And that's good news.

How long can you hold your breath? People cannot live long without air. Plants, animals, and people breathe air to stay alive.

Air surrounds Earth. ▶

Think of all the ways you use air:
    for breathing,
    for blowing bubbles,
    for filling balloons,
    for listening.

Often you cannot see it or feel it.
But air shapes our lives.

How Heat Changes Air

Air is always a gas. But air changes when it heats each day and cools each night.

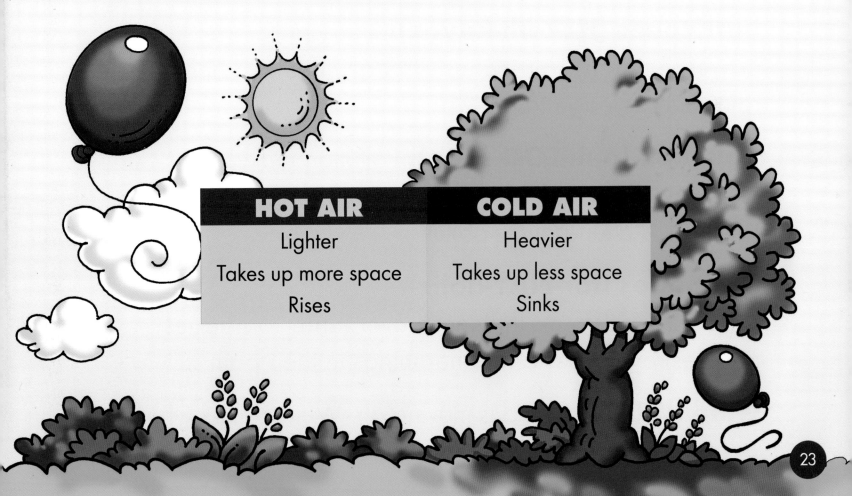

HOT AIR	COLD AIR
Lighter	Heavier
Takes up more space	Takes up less space
Rises	Sinks

Words to Know

gas (GAS): A gas is something that flows like water but spreads to fill any container. Air is a gas.

hurricanes (HER-uh-kaynz): Hurricanes are powerful storms. Hurricanes' strong winds and heavy rains can damage towns.

pollution (puh-LOO-shun): Pollution makes air and water dirty and harmful to the planet. Smoke from factories is a kind of air pollution.

tornadoes (tor-NAY-dohz): Tornadoes are spinning windstorms that move over land. Tornadoes can destroy houses and other things in their path.

wind (WIND): Wind is moving air. Wind comes when warm air moves up and colder air rushes in below.